CAT NAPS

Published by Sellers Publishing, Inc.

161 John Roberts Road, South Portland, ME 04106
Visit us at www.sellerspublishing.com • E-mail: rsp@rsvp.com

Copyright © 2015 Sellers Publishing, Inc.
All rights reserved.

Compiled by Robin Haywood

ISBN: 978-1-4162-4569-8

Printed and bound in China.

Cover image © 2015 Cindy Pitts
Credits appear on page 128.

10 9 8 7 6 5 4 3 2 1

CAT NAPS

THE KEY TO CONTENTMENT

SELLERS
PUBLISHING

Life is hard,
then you nap.

Anonymous

The idea of calm
exists in a sitting cat.

Jules Renard

How beautiful it is to do nothing,
and then to rest afterward.

Spanish proverb

There is more to life
than increasing its speed.

Mohandas Gandhi

I don't know why it is
we are in such a hurry
to get up when we fall
down. You might think
we would lie there and
rest awhile.

Max Forrester Eastman

If there were to be
a universal sound
depicting peace,
I would surely vote
for the purr.

Barbara L. Diamond

If I didn't wake up,
I'd still be sleeping!

Yogi Berra

Light be the earth upon you,
lightly rest.

Euripides

Learning to ignore things is one of the great paths to inner peace.

Robert J. Sawyer

The best cure
for insomnia is
to get a lot of sleep.

W. C. Fields

Champagne wishes
and caviar dreams . . .

Anonymous

Cats are rather delicate creatures and they are subject to a good many ailments, but I never heard of one who suffered from insomnia.

Joseph Wood Krutch

A cat pours his
body on the
floor like water.
It is restful just
to see him.

William Lyon Phelps

I have never taken
any exercise except
sleeping and resting.

Mark Twain (Samuel L. Clemens)

Who among us hasn't envied a cat's ability to ignore the cares of daily life and to relax completely?

Karen Brademeyer

A well-spent
day brings a
happy sleep.

Leonardo da Vinci

The secret of happiness
is to make others believe
they are the cause of it.

Al Batt

Oh sleep! It is a gentle thing,
Beloved from pole to pole.

Samuel Taylor Coleridge

Slow down and enjoy life.
It's not only the scenery
you miss by going too fast
– you also miss the sense
of where you are going
and why.

Eddie Cantor

Sleep is the best meditation.

Tenzin Gyatso,
the 14th Dalai Lama

There's never enough time to do all the nothing you want.

Bill Watterson

Loafing needs no explanation
and is its own excuse.

Christopher Morley

Yawn and the world
yawns with you.
Snore and you
sleep alone.

Anonymous

When the going gets tough, the tough take a nap.

Tom Hodgkinson

There is more refreshment and stimulation in a nap, even of the briefest, than in all the alcohol ever distilled.

Edward Lucas

53

No day is so bad
it can't be fixed
with a nap.

Carrie Snow

When you can't figure out what to do,
it's time for a nap.

Mason Cooley

Very little is needed
to make a happy life.

Marcus Aurelius Antoninus

Taking a nap,
feet planted
against a cool wall.

Matsuo Basho

If there is one spot
of sun spilling onto
the floor, a cat will
find it and soak it up.

Jean Asper McIntosh

Life is too short
to sleep on low
thread-count
sheets.

Leah Stussy

Slow down and everything you are
chasing will come around and catch you.

John DePaola

The fog comes
on little cat feet.

Carl Sandburg

Subliminal kitty messages? "You are getting very sleepy" is not a command when said to a cat; it is an eternal truth.

Ari Ripkin

Follow your bliss and doors will open where there were no doors before.

Joseph Campbell

Kittens are born with their eyes shut. They open them in about six days, take a look around, then close them again for the better part of their lives.

Stephen Baker

The time to relax is when you don't have time for it.

Author unknown

. . . there is a luxury in being quiet in the heart of chaos.

Virginia Woolf

Everything I know
I learned from my cat:
When you're hungry, eat.
When you're tired,
nap in a sunbeam.
When you go to the vet's,
pee on your owner.

Gary Smith

There is no need to go to India or anywhere else to find peace. You will find that deep place of silence right in your room, your garden, or even your bathtub.

Dr. Elisabeth Kübler-Ross, M.D.

A little drowsing cat is an image of perfect beatitude.

Jules Champfleury

Don't underestimate
the value of doing nothing,
of just going along, listening
to all the things you can't
hear, and not bothering.

A. A. Milne

To sleep is
an act of faith.

Barbara G. Harrison

He seems the incarnation of everything soft and silky and velvety, without a sharp edge in his composition, a dreamer whose philosophy is sleep and let sleep.

Saki (H. H. Munro)

Now I see the secret of the making of the best persons. It is to grow in the open air and to eat and sleep with the earth.

Walt Whitman

It takes a lot of courage
to show your dreams
to someone else.

Erma Bombeck

Festinalente:
Make haste slowly.

Prowling his own quiet backyard or asleep by the fire, he is still only a whisker away from the wilds.

Jean Burden

The future belongs to those who believe
in the beauty of their dreams.

Eleanor Roosevelt

Rest is not idleness,
and to lie sometimes
on the grass under trees
on a summer's day,
listening to the murmur
of the water, or watching
the clouds float across
the sky, is by no means
a waste of time.

John Lubbock

Which is more beautiful:
feline movement
or feline stillness?

Elizabeth Hamilton

A good laugh and
a long sleep are
the best cures in
the doctor's book.

Irish proverb

Cats are
connoisseurs
of comfort.

James Herriot

Laziness works. And the simple way to incorporate its health benefits into your life is simply to take a nap.

Tom Hodgkinson

Nap like no one
is listening.
Nap like you've
never been hurt.
Nap like nobody
is watching.

Patricia Robinson

113

I don't look for bliss, just contentment.

Alison Krauss

Work less than you think
you should. It took me a
while to realize there was
a point each day when my
creativity ran out and I was
just producing words —
usually lousy ones — for
their own sake. And nap:
it helps to refresh the brain,
at least mine.

Amy Waldman

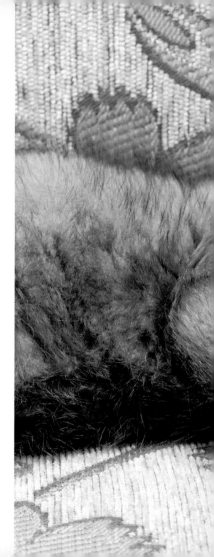

A day without
a nap is like a
cupcake without
frosting.

Terri Guillemets

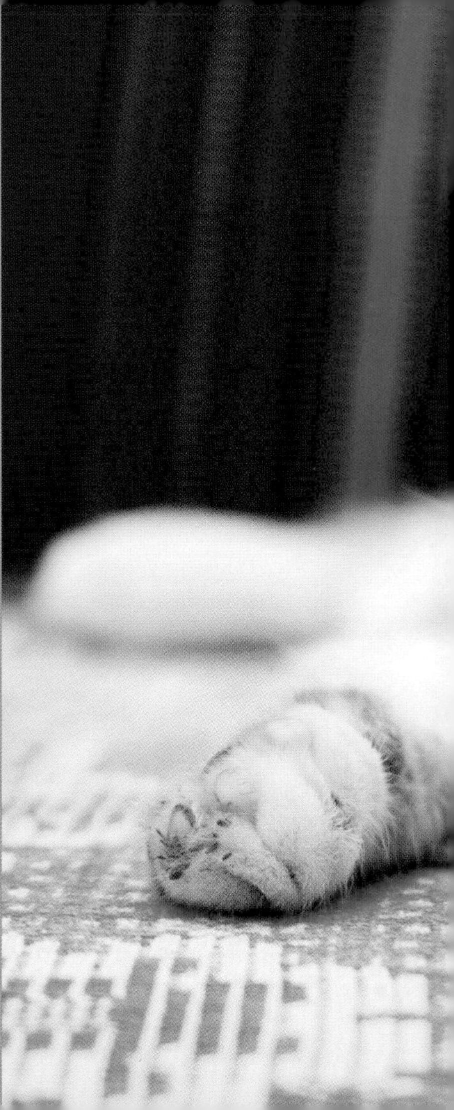

Be content with what you have; rejoice in the way things are. When you realize there is nothing lacking, the whole world belongs to you.

Lao Tzu

At some point, you gotta let go and sit still and allow contentment to come to you.

Elizabeth Gilbert

A contented mind
is the greatest
blessing a person
can enjoy in this
world.

Joseph Addison

He is rich who
is content with
the least; for
contentment is
the wealth of
nature.

Socrates

Credits:

Cover photo: © Cindy Pitts.

Front cover flap photo: © vita khorzhevska/Shutterstock.

p. 3 photo © KPG Payless/Shutterstock; pp. 4-5 photo © AAresTT/Shutterstock; pp. 6-7 photo © Dziewul/Shutterstock; pp. 8-9 photo © Evgenia Bolyukh/Shutterstock; pp. 10-11 photo © KPG Payless/Shutterstock; pp. 12-13 photo © MonsterSpace/Shutterstock; pp. 14-15 photo © Ermolaev Alexander/Shutterstock; pp. 16-17 photo © Dalibor Valek/Shutterstock; pp. 18-19 photo © Grisha Bruev/Shutterstock; pp. 20-21 photo © Denis and Yulia Pogostins; pp. 22-23 photo © MaxyM/Shutterstock; pp. 24-25 photo © Alena Ozerova/Shutterstock; pp. 26-27 photo © DreamBig/Shutterstock; pp. 28-29 photo © Pakhnyushchy/Shutterstock; pp. 30-31 photo © Gita Kulinitch Studio/Shutterstock; p. 32 photo © Cindy Pitts; pp. 34-35 photo © ArtShotPhoto/Shutterstock; pp. 36-37 photo © Fri9thsep/Shutterstock; pp. 38-39 photo © Littlesam/Shutterstock; pp. 40-41 photo © Haru/Shutterstock; pp. 42-43 photo © Jianghaistudio/Shutterstock; pp. 44-45 photo © Marahwan/Shutterstock; p. 45 Bill Watterson from *Calvin and Hobbes*; pp. 46-47 photo © Dora Zett/Shutterstock; pp. 48-49 photo © Olena2552/Shutterstock; pp. 50-51 photo © Yusia/Shutterstock; pp. 52-53 photo © Berna Namoglu/Shutterstock; pp. 54-55 photo © Tkemot/Shutterstock; pp. 56-57 photo © Africa Studio/Shutterstock; pp. 58-59 photo © Goran Cakmazovic/Shutterstock; p. 60 photo © Vinogradov Illya/Shutterstock; p. 61 Matsuo Basho, "Taking a Nap"; pp. 62-63 photo © FotomanX/Shutterstock; pp. 64-65 photo © Oleg Kozlov/Shutterstock; pp. 66-67 photo © Patpitchaya/Shutterstock; pp. 68-69 © Larisa Lofitskaya/Shutterstock; p. 69 Carl Sandburg from "The Fog;" pp. 70-71 photo © Andrey Kuzmin/Shutterstock; pp. 72-73 photo © Julija Sapic/Shutterstock; pp. 74-75 photo © Tony Campbell/Shutterstock; pp. 76-77 photo © KobchaiMa/Shutterstock; pp. 78-79 photo © Alexander Mazurkevich/Shutterstock; pp. 80-81 photo © Pashin Georgiy/Shutterstock; pp. 82-83 photo © Berna Namoglu/Shutterstock; pp. 84-85 photo © TalyaPhoto/Shutterstock; pp. 86-87 photo © Vasilev Evgenii/Shutterstock; p. 87 A. A. Milne from *Pooh's Little Instruction Book*; pp. 88-89 photo © Berna Namoglu/Shutterstock; pp. 90-91 photo © Vita Khorzhevska/Shutterstock; pp. 92-93 photo © DavidTB/Shutterstock; p. 92 Walt Whitman from *Song of the Open Road*; pp. 94-95 photo © VladimirE/Shutterstock; pp. 96-97 photo © Vera Kailova/Shutterstock; pp. 98-99 photo © TalyaPhoto/Shutterstock; pp. 100-101 photo © Juhku/Shutterstock; pp. 102-103 photo © Aastock/Shutterstock; pp. 104-105 photo © Milosz G/Shutterstock; pp. 106-107 photo © Taisa/Shutterstock; pp. 108-109 © Linn Currie/Shutterstock; pp. 110-111 photo © Birute Vijeikiene/Shutterstock; pp. 112-113 photo © Liliya Kulianionak/Shutterstock; pp. 114-115 photo © Bonchan/Shutterstock; pp. 116-117 photo © Plus69/Shutterstock; pp. 118-119 photo © TalyaPhoto/Shutterstock; pp. 120-121 photo © Phadungsak Sawasdee/Shutterstock; pp. 122-123 photo © Choikh/Shutterstock; pp. 124-125 photo © Andrey Kuzmin/Shutterstock; pp. 126-127 photo © Liliya Kulianionak/Shutterstock.